Beneath Our Feet - volume 1
ISBN 9798850375409
First Printing, 2023

Each detectorist supplied their own photos, bios, and descriptions, which are used with their permission. Wood/sand/beach background images, as well as country flag icons, are licensed stock photography images used within licensing guidelines.

I would like to express my heartfelt gratitude to all the detectorists who have eagerly contributed to this book. The wonderful discoveries you've made and the captivating stories you've shared have truly enriched its content. Thank you for being a part of this incredible journey!

All the finds celebrated in this book are "natural" finds. Nothing contained in these pages is from a seeded hunt.

Do you have an amazing find you would like celebrated in a future volume of Beneath Our Feet? If so, send an email to ken@detectorist.com and include a short description of the find along with a photo.

Printed in the United States of America.

BENEATH OUR FEET

volume 1

KEN CUNLIFFE

TABLE OF CONTENTS

(alphabetical order by first name)

TABLE OF CONTENTS
(continued)

FOREWORD

As a detectorist I am both humbled and thrilled to be included in this book. The author has assembled a wonderful collection of very interesting people and their recoveries. Men and women, young and old, diverse individuals from around the world, we all share the dream and passion of finding something lost long ago. It's part of our psyche. It's embedded in our DNA. It is what we think about constantly. We are curious creatures, and we want to know the history behind everything we find. And we delight in sharing that information with anyone who will listen. We detect, we dig, and we get dirty...a lot. But for us, it is absolutely worth the time and effort. For a moment in time, finding something satisfies us, and then it's time to start searching again.

The truth is we are just temporary stewards of everything we find. And everything we find has a story. And one day those stories will be lost or forgotten. That's why this book is so important. It captures the essence of each person and the finds they share within these pages. This is just the beginning. There are so many other folks whose stories deserve to be told and their finds documented. That's why I am encouraging the author to continue with volume two and beyond. I hope you enjoy reading this book as much as I enjoyed contributing to it.

Finally, I encourage everyone to read and contemplate Ken's introduction. It paints a wonderful portrait of who we are and why we look for things beneath our feet.

Marc Hoover
Adventures In History

INTRODUCTION

Have you ever wondered what lies beneath the surface of the ground we walk upon? What lost treasures, long-forgotten relics, and stories of the past are waiting to be discovered? The hobby of metal detecting holds the key to unlocking a world of wonders buried beneath our feet. It is a pursuit that connects us to history in a profound and tangible way, weaving a thread through time and allowing detectorists to become time travelers.

In the quiet solitude of early mornings or the golden hues of sunset, detectorists embark on a journey of exploration and curiosity. Armed with their trusty metal detectors, they traverse fields, beaches, forests, and forgotten homes, searching for echoes of the past. With each swing of the coil, a symphony of beeps and chirps, a language only they can decipher, reveals the presence of buried artifacts and lost treasures.

But metal detecting is more than just a hobby—it is a window into the stories and lives of those who walked the same paths we tread today. With every unearthed coin, button, relic, or lost ring, we are transported back in time, connecting with the intricate tapestry of human existence. It is a thrill that stirs the soul and ignites the fervor of detectorists around the world.

Imagine the joy of discovering a Roman coin, an item from a civilization that thrived many centuries ago. Contemplate the weight of history as you hold in your hands an axe head, crafted by an ancient hunter on a quest for survival. Feel the whispers of a bygone era as you unearth a wartime medal, a poignant reminder of the sacrifice and resilience of generations past. These artifacts are not mere trinkets—they are gateways to a world long gone, beckoning us to uncover its secrets.

With each find, we become part of a vast network of individuals connected through the shared wonder of discovery. We pour over historical records, maps, and books, researching and understanding the context of our finds. We gather in local clubs, online forums, and at

INTRODUCTION
(continued)

organized events, exchanging stories, knowledge, and expertise. We are united in our passion for uncovering the past and preserving its memory.

However, metal detecting is not without its challenges and ethical responsibilities. Detectorists understand the importance of responsible digging, leaving no trace behind, and obtaining proper permissions to search on private lands. We recognize the significance of preserving archaeological sites, collaborating with professionals, and reporting significant discoveries to protect our shared heritage.

Within these pages, we celebrate incredible finds unearthed by passionate detectorists around the world, offering a glimpse into the hidden treasures that lie beneath our feet.

Ken Cunliffe
Detectorist.com

ADAM GUIEL

Bio: Adam lives in Shropshire, England and started detecting in 2006. He uses the XP Deus but started out with the Garrett Euro-Ace. He has had several finds in local museums but is now using them for school visits. Owner of @d3tectartist and handsonhistory.org.

Find Info: Silver Roman Republican denarius serratus, Rome, 83 BC, Quintus Antonius Balbus (moneyer), RRC 364/1c. Obverse has laureate head of Jupiter facing right with S•C behind. Reverse has Victory in quadriga driving right, holding a branch and wreath.

Silver Roman Republican Denarius
83BC

BRAD JOHNS

Bio: Brad is from Maryland and is currently hunting with the Minelab Equinox 800, Garrett AT Max, and Fisher F75. He is a coin and jewelry enthusiast and a treasure hunter from birth.

Find Info: If you have ever heard someone say, "Oh my gosh, I flowing haired it" in response to damaging a find, it's because of this coin, which I unfortunately nicked with my shovel back in the spring of 2017. It is the sweetest little coin I never expected to find, and it was a whirlwind of emotions finding it! I remember it like it was yesterday, and the video footage still takes my breath away.

1795 Flowing Hair
Half Dime

BRAD MARTIN

Bio: Brad Martin lives in Vermont and is currently using the XP Deus II. He explores the mountains of Vermont in search of the treasures lost by the pioneers who lived there before him and films the adventures for his YouTube channel – Green Mountain Metal Detecting.

Find Info: Silver Pendant inscribed "Miss Anna A Leonard – Born May 5th, 1794". Found in the ruins of a Vermont mountain stagecoach stop. Anna was born in Conway, MA but moved to Dexter, MI around 1820, where she raised a family and eventually died in 1872. Her full story can be seen on YouTube in "The Story of Anna & the Pendant."

Inscribed Silver Pendant
"Miss Anna A Leonard"

BRANDON RAY NEICE

Bio: Brandon lives and detects in the Pacific Northwest of America. Aside from treasure hunting, Brandon enjoys video production, which has contributed to his YouTube channel, "DrTones24k." Throughout his treasure hunting career, he has traveled far and wide, finding an impressive array of coins, relics, gold nuggets, and even meteorites. His passion for the hobby inspired him to share his knowledge through his first and second edition bestselling books, "The Metal Detecting Bible."

Find Info: Pictured is one of many silver hammered coins I recovered that are part of the "Shropshire Short Cross Hoard" dating from 1189-1216. This coin holds a special place in my heart because of the unique moneyer mark bearing my son's name, "Abel." I remember holding that coin in my hand, thinking, "WOW! What are the odds of me finding a coin of this age with my son's name on it?"

22

"Shropshire Short Cross Hoard"
Silver Penny (1189-1216)

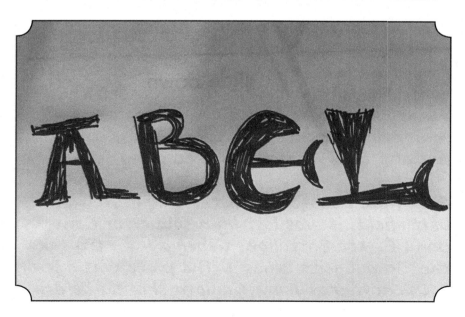

BUTCH HOLCOMBE

Bio: Butch is from Marietta, Georgia. He has been detecting since 1968, starting with a Heathkit he built with his dad. He founded American Digger magazine (americandigger. com) 19 years ago and has expanded the American Digger brand to also include two major annual artifact shows each year. Butch has also authored several detecting books.

Find Info: Recovered on the Gilgal Church battlefield, it was lost by a soldier of Company C, 1st Battalion, Georgia Infantry (aka the "Republican Blues"). The plate was one of 1,000 ordered from Gaylord shortly before the war and is considered extremely rare.

Georgia Militia
Cartridge Box Plate

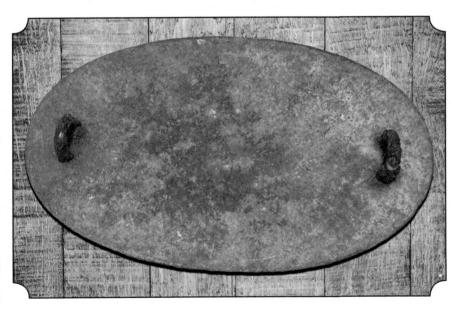

CHRIS HOFFERT

Bio: Chris is from Manheim, Pennsylvania. He hunts primarily with a Minelab Equinox 800 and has been detecting for about 15 years, focusing on colonial and Civil War artifacts. Chris achieved his greatest find when he proposed to his wife by burying the engagement ring on his property in upstate New York.

Find Info: Union NCO (Non-Commissioned Officer) Sword Sash Breast Plate. Recovered in April 2023 near the Battle of Freeman's Ford in Remington, Virginia, on the last day of DIV 54. The backside has three hooks instead of the typical two, signifying that it belonged to a Union officer for use in an over-the-shoulder sword belt.

Union Officer Sword
Sash Breast Plate

CHRIS LANGSTON

Bio: Chris lives and detects on the border of England and Wales in Shropshire, England. He detects solo and is part of "Team Regton" metal detectors and "Team Garrett" UK and USA metal detectors. Chris also has a popular Instagram page where you can see some of the incredible finds he has made! Search Instagram: @metaldetectingholidays.

Find Info: Henry VI Gold Noble 1422–1427 AD Annulet Issue – Calais Mint (North: 1415) (Spink 1799). Recorded with the Shropshire FLO on the PAS website www.pas.org.uk. Found in 2021 in Shropshire, England, with the Garrett AT Max and Garrett Raider Coil.

1422-1427 Henry VI
Gold Noble

CLEM CHAMBERS

Bio: Known as Chill Bill, a YouTuber, treasure hunter, and mudlarker based in Monaco, he uses an XP Deus with the HF coil because he feels it is one of the lightest and most sensitive detectors around. His YouTube channel can be found by searching "Chill Bill Treasure," and he has collaborated with many other YouTubers.

Find Info: Roman key, second century AD. The key was found while I was looking for a farmer's hammer, on its own in the middle of an empty field. Apart from being a wonderful, rare, large, ancient bronze item that is well-preserved, it leaves me wondering if the chest it unlocked is nearby.

Roman Key
Second Century AD

DAN KNIGHT

Bio: Dan Knight, aged 61, is from Camden County, New Jersey. He has been metal detecting since the late 70s. Dan hunts ocean beaches, lakes, and Civil War relics using a Deus, T2, and Excalibur.

Find Info: Recovered near the James River outside of Petersburg, VA, the special water cap fuse failed to explode while passing over a Confederate fort. As a result, 75 pounds of cast-iron (and 5 pounds of black powder) remained intact. It has now been safely disarmed and preserved. Research indicates that it was likely fired in July 1862 by the Union river gunboat USS Sebago, the only ship with that type and diameter of gun known to have bombarded the site.

Naval "Dahlgren" Shell
9 Inch

DAVE ROSE

Bio: Dave lives in southwest Illinois and started detecting in 1977. He currently uses the XP Deus II and a Minelab E-Trac. He considers himself fortunate to have had the opportunity to go metal detecting in England and Germany on many occasions.

Find Info: Dates to the Hallstatt Culture (c. 12th to 8th century BCE), this religious offering could have been made for various reasons, such as a prayer for a healthy baby or abundant crops. It was recovered in Bavaria near the base of a 60-foot natural stone cliff face (shown in the photo). Among the other items found in the offering were a single bronze ring (ring money) and two round pieces of bronze casting waste.

Bronze Age Votive Offering
(c. 12th to 8th century BCE)

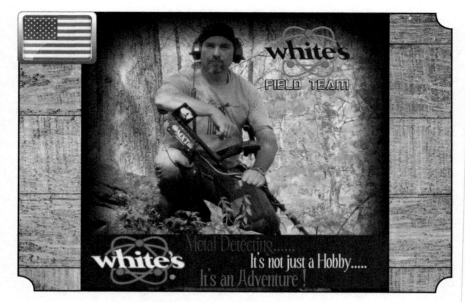

DAVE WISE

Bio: Dave Wise lives in Waterbury, Connecticut, and hunts with a White's MXT All Pro. Dave is a content creator on his YouTube channel "heavymetalnut1965". He feels blessed to be able to hunt colonial cellar holes in Connecticut and save so much history that has ties to the birth of our nation.

Find Info: My favorite find is my first George Washington Inaugural Button from 1789. The variety is the oval with GW in the center and "Long Live The President" around the perimeter. Since that first button, I have dug 12 more GW buttons, all eagle with star varieties. That makes a total of 13 GW buttons, one for each of the original 13 colonies!

1789 George Washington Inaugural Button

GEORGE WASHINGTON INAUGURAL BUTTONS 1789

DAWN CHIPCHASE

Bio: Dawn lives in Lancashire, England. She has been metal detecting for 8 years and uses the Garrett AT Max and the Garrett Apex. She is part of "Team Regton" metal detectors based in the UK and "Team Garrett" UK & USA. Also known as Digger Dawn, she has a YouTube channel with 26K subscribers and a large following across other social media platforms, including Facebook (35K) and Instagram (7K).

Find Info: Roman Silver Denarius. Emperor Trajan 98-118 AD. Obverse: laureate bust right, drapery on left shoulder. Reverse: Aequitas standing left, holding scales and Cornucopia.

Roman Silver Denarius
Emperor Trajan (98-118AD)

DEBBIE SCHIFFER-BLADES

Bio: Debbie lives in the Missouri Ozarks and hunts with an Equinox 800 and an AT Max. She is the secretary of the Laclede County Treasure Trackers metal detecting club. Additionally, she is a published author, proofreader, and has recently become a copy editor for American Digger magazine.

Find Info: I was astounded when a professional analysis revealed the origin of my find to be the Ming Dynasty era (1400s). This remarkable revelation has garnered attention from a renowned Chinese scholar who has approached me with an extraordinary opportunity: to showcase the artifact in the esteemed Palace Museum in China.

Chinese Ring
Ming Dynasty (1400s)

DENNIS PEACOCK

Bio: Dennis lives in Scituate, Massachusetts, and hunts with an Equinox 800 and Deus II. He spends long hours researching and documenting 17th-century sites, many of which were previously unknown. Searching for these sites and sharing his passion with friends is as rewarding as the thrill of any individual discovery... almost.

Find Info: Found at a 17th-century trade site, Tree Coins are universally regarded as the most highly prized detecting finds among Colonial American relics. This beautiful example, a NOE-36 variety, boasts AU details and tremendous visual appeal.

Pine Tree Threepence
1652

DONNIE BAILEY

Bio: Donnie has been detecting in the Eastern United States for more than 27 years. He detects for the same reason as most detectorists: the love of history. When not detecting, you can usually find him studying history, researching sites for detecting, or time traveling. He has written several articles for Western & Eastern Treasures.

Find Info: There are quite a few different varieties of Massachusetts silver coins. Mine is a Noe-16 (Salmon 2-B) Small Planchet Pine Tree Shilling. It is almost full "standard legal weight" at 70.1 grains. I found the coin in Connecticut while detecting with one of my best friends. I will never forget that day.

Massachusetts Bay Colony
1652 Pine Tree Shilling

DREW WAINACHT

Bio: Drew Wainacht is from Putnam, Connecticut, and hunts with the XP Deus II. Drew, also known as "OxShoeDrew," is an administrator at AmericanDetectorist.com. As a recently retired teacher, Drew gets to begin each day with a short hunt.

Find Info: One of my favorite finds is this silver trade brooch, possibly from the 13th century. To find anything this old in New England is rare and may be evidence of contact between Europeans and indigenous people much earlier than previously thought. It was found near a known sacred Native American gathering place.

Native American
Silver Trade Brooch

ED HUFFMAN

Bio: Ed is from Melissa, Texas, and hunts with a Garrett AT MAX. He has been metal detecting for more than 30 years and is a content creator on his YouTube channel, Adventures With Ed Huffman. His remarkable discoveries have earned him features in numerous metal detecting books and magazines, showcasing the diverse range of treasures he has unearthed during his thrilling expeditions

Find Info: I found this halfpenny at an area in Williamsburg, Virginia, that I researched to have Revolutionary and Civil War activity. Virginia was just one of the thirteen colonies in 1773, and it became the 10th state in 1778.

Virginia Halfpenny
1773

FRED BANKE

Bio: He lives in Micco, Florida, and detects Florida's Treasure Coast and the Indian Wars of the Northern Plains. He has written and published two books on metal detecting the Treasure Coast and one on the Indian Wars. Fred is a guest speaker at local museums and high schools. He also serves as a tour guide at the Mel Fisher Treasure Museum. Currently, he is using the Manticore and Nokta Legend detectors. His website is therealedeal.com.

Find Info: Religious artifact believed to be from a 1600s Spanish shipwreck. The object is bronze, made up of copper, tin, and a small amount of silver. It is crudely cast and 9k gold-plated.

Religious Artifact
(1600s)

GARETH JONES

Bio: Gareth comes from a small medieval market town called Ellesmere, Shropshire, in England. He uses the Garrett Ace 400i and the Garrett Ace Apex detectors.

Find Info: Copper Medieval Royal Crown Seal Matrix - circa 1101-1263. Recovered close to a castle in Shropshire, this seal matrix features a royal crown and was used to seal important documents from the local castle (built in 1086). In 1101, the castle and land were taken over by the Crown and made into a royal castle until 1263. The castle was destroyed during the Civil War and turned into a bowling green in the 18th century.

Medieval Royal Crown Seal
1101–1263

GARETH MILLWARD

Bio: Gareth is an avid metal detectorist from Chesterfield, England. He is 41 years old and has been metal detecting for more than 8 years. Gareth is currently using the XP Deus II detector. He also runs a YouTube channel and an Instagram account, both called "The Dukes of Derbyshire."

Find Info: Georgian gold FOB seal (1750-1820). This beautiful seal was recovered under a tree in a pasture field in front of a Georgian Manor in Derbyshire, England, in November 2019. Made of gold, with a Griffin intaglio, it is one of the most stunning things I've ever been lucky enough to unearth.

Georgian Gold FOB Seal
1750-1820

GARY E. KILLMER

Bio: Gary is from LaGrange, New York. He has been detecting since 1984 and currently hunts with the XP Deus II. Gary has also used Minelab detectors for many years. In the past, he worked on assembling early Minelab Excaliburs and Grey Ghost headphones.

Find Info: A 3000-5000-year-old copper adze, attached to a wooden handle, used for shaping wood. This ancient find impressed the Curator of Archaeology at the NYS Museum. It was discovered along a stream in the Hudson Valley and is most likely a traded item from the Mid-West or a much further northern region where natural copper deposits exist.

Copper Adze
(3000–5000 years old)

GENE WALTER

Bio: Gene is from Columbia, PA, and hunts with various detectors, including the AT Pro, CTX 3030, and the Manticore. He holds the position of President at Lancaster Research and Recovery Club (LRRC.Org). Gene has provided valuable assistance to archaeologists at Camp Security in their search for a Revolutionary War Prison Camp Stockade.

Find Info: This is my first and only silver dollar find in 12 years of detecting. I was on a site that yielded 20-plus coppers for my hunting partner. We were about to leave, and I said I was going to dig one more hole. That hole had this beautiful lady hiding among several nails.

1798 Draped Bust
Silver Dollar

GEORGE WYANT

Bio: George Wyant (aka King George), of National Geographic's "DIGGERS" and the Pursuit channel's "DIGGIN with KG & RINGY," has been a treasure hunter for almost 20 years. As part of Team Garrett, he and his TV co-star Ringmaster Tim continue to search for treasures worldwide, with multiple museum contributions in England, Europe, and the USA. Their exploits, documented in over 85 television shows, countless YouTube videos, touring events, and a live podcast series, can all be referenced at DIGGINTV.com.

Find Info: An extremely rare Civil War-era railroad baggage tag was found with a Garrett AT MAX on an old plantation in Louisiana. The USMRR (US Military Railroad) was a wartime entity that existed only from 1862 to 1865.

Civil War era
Railroad Baggage Tag

GYPSY JEWELS

Bio: Gypsy is a resident of Texas and uses a Garrett Apex and the Garrett AT Max. She is an expert field team member with Garrett Metal Detectors, a treasure hunting TV show guest consultant, YouTube host, and podcast co-host. Notable appearances include "Beyond Oak Island" and "Gold Rush." Be sure to check out her website at GypsyDigs.com.

Find Info: The "I" on the button indicates that the wearer was an infantry soldier. This beautiful button was recovered from a cornfield in Maine with my Garrett Apex, equipped with a 5x8 Ripper coil in multiple frequency mode, and set to ZERO DISCRIMINATION.

Civil War Infantry Button
(ca. 1861)

HENRY PARRO

Bio: Henry is from Waterbury, Vermont. He started detecting in the early '70s and currently uses a Deus II. Henry hunts in the New England area and travels to England in the spring. He values the friendships he has made in the detecting community. Henry is a member of Diggin' in VA, and several of his finds have been featured in books, including Andy Sabisch's book on the first Deus, "I'll Take a Button Over a Coin Any Day."

Find Info: Gaul, Ambiani or Nervii Quarter Stater (175 BC). This extremely rare coin has only twenty known examples. Once it was returned to me via the export process, I had it graded and slabbed.

Gaul, Ambiani or Nervii
Quarter Stater (175BC)

HENRY SMITH

Bio: Henry Smith (aka Hank) is from Pitman, New Jersey. He took up metal detecting as a hobby in his late 30s and is currently using an XP Deus. Hank feels fortunate to live in the northeastern US, which is so rich in history. He has also traveled to Colchester, England, to metal detect.

Find Info: I recovered this on the edge of a farm field in New Jersey while pulling a bunch of half cents and large cents. Honestly, I thought it was just a large washer, but as I tried to push the dirt from the center, I saw a head. I've kept it in my display exactly as I found it, never cleaned. It's a tarnished, dinged, yet priceless treasure!

1821 Fernando VII
8 Reales

JAKE CARROLL

Bio: Jake Carroll, 23 years old, is from O'Fallon, Missouri. His detector of choice is the Garrett AT Pro. Jake started detecting at age 14 and immediately became hooked. Recovering colonial and Civil War relics is his favorite. He has detected in the United States as well as England.

Find Info: Civil War Confederate States Officer's Buckle. Recovered in 2018 in Amherst, Virginia, at a colonial site. It seems that a small Confederate troop must have camped on the land, as several bullets and other Civil War artifacts were found among the colonial relics.

Civil War
Confederate States Officer's Buckle

JAMES MAURO

Bio: James is from Somers, Connecticut, and hunts with an Equinox 600. As a kid, his friend found a 1788 Massachusetts copper in a dirt pile, which sparked an interest in metal detecting that he wouldn't fully pursue until 2013. His Instagram account is @Dirty_Relics, and he had a find featured in Western & Eastern Treasures.

Find Info: The New York Militia Excelsior Officer's Belt Plate was recovered in 2015 in Tolland County, Connecticut. It was once worn by a lieutenant of the 171st Regiment, New York Militia, circa 1830–1850.

New York Militia Excelsior
Officer's Belt Plate

JAY VERBURG

Bio: Jay Verburg is from Red Creek, New York. He hunts with the Minelab Equinox 800 and XP Deus II detectors. Jay has been detecting for 13 years now and absolutely loves this hobby. He has formed great friendships and traveled to amazing places to metal detect.

Find Info: Celtic Gold Full Stater, 50 BC, Middle Whaddon Chase. Obverse: Cross of 3 plain and 2 pellet lines with 2 opposed crescents b in center. Reverse: Horse r. above pellet in ring, pellet in wheel below. VA 1491, BMC 343, ABC. Recovered in Essex, England.

Celtic Gold Full Stater
50BC

JEFF HETHERINGTON

Bio: Jeff lives in the Niagara Region of Southern Ontario, Canada. He bought his first metal detector in 2007 and enjoys traveling to England and the United States to metal detect. His metal detector of choice is the Minelab Equinox 800.

Find Info: My favorite find is a gold half sovereign. This 1853 half sovereign features the Young Head design of Queen Victoria on the obverse, and the reverse displays the shield design. There is no mint mark, indicating that this coin was produced at the London Mint.

Gold Half Sovereign
1853

JEFF LUTZ

Bio: Jeff is from Powersville, MO. He hunts with a Minelab Manticore and has been detecting for more than 50 years. Jeff loves relic hunting with an emphasis on the Civil War. Jeff and his wife have traveled to England and hunted in Colchester, the oldest town in England. They have been fortunate to find artifacts from the Stone Age, Bronze Age, Celtic, Roman, Saxon, and Medieval periods.

Find Info: I have chosen a Civil War 1851 Officer's Eagle Belt Plate as my favorite find. I was lucky enough to find both pieces of the belt plate, 10 years apart, within 250 yards of each other.

Officer's Eagle Belt Plate
1851

JEFF PELLETIER

Bio: Jeff is from Bristol, Connecticut. He has been metal detecting for over 30 years and uses a Minelab CTX 3030, Excalibur II, and the Manticore. Jeff has had his finds featured in many books, newspapers, and magazines. He is a member of four metal detecting clubs in Connecticut and New York.

Find Info: Found in Salisbury, Connecticut, on a field I had driven by for years. One day, I saw someone pulling into the property, and after a short conversation, I received a one-time permission. This button came out of the ground with all the silver plating and amazing details. It was in perfect condition!

War of 1812 Infantry Officer's Button "The Grey Ghost"

JIM TIPPITT

Bio: Jim is also known as "Jimmy Crossbones" and lives in New Smyrna Beach, Florida. Jim is a distant cousin of Davy Crockett, a popular hero of American folklore from Tennessee. Jim is the President of the Central Florida Metal Detecting Club, one of the oldest and largest metal detecting clubs in the U.S. He uses a Minelab CTX 3030 and Equinox 800. His YouTube channel is JIMMY CROSSBONES.

Find Info: "Jimmy Crossbones Treasure" – recovered in 2018 on a beach on the East Coast of Florida. This treasure was a very small part of what was lost by a fleet of eleven Spanish galleons that sank during a hurricane off the coast of Florida on July 31st, 1715. The treasure consists of four gold 8-escudos, nine gold 2-escudos, one silver 8-reale, twenty-seven silver 2-reales, six silver half-reales, one gold cuff link, one small gold ring, and dozens of other Spanish shipwreck artifacts. 80

Gold Cuff Link – part of the "Jimmy Crossbones Treasure"

JOHN QUINN

Bio: John Quinn, retired USAF, is from Swansea, Illinois. He has been metal detecting for more than 27 years and hunts in the United States, Japan, and the United Kingdom. John is proud to have several coins on display in a UK museum.

Find Info: 1643 King Charles I hammered half crown. This coin was recovered in 2019 in the United Kingdom. This coin was only the second of its type ever found in the area around Colchester, England. After 27 years of metal detecting, this coin is special to me as it is the first hammered coin I ever recovered.

1643 King Charles I
Hammered Half Crown

KELLY CARROLL

Bio: Kelly Carroll is from O'Fallon, Missouri, and she hunts with an Equinox 600. Kelly started metal detecting to share a hobby with her teenage son, and they have been detecting together for close to 10 years, both loving it. She recently purchased a home on the Treasure Coast to begin beach detecting.

Find Info: My favorite find is this Republic of Texas Dragoon Military button, which was recovered in 2019 in Foristell, Missouri. Finding this rare button in the middle of Missouri was a wonderful surprise!

Republic of Texas
Dragoon Military Button

KEN CUNLIFFE

Bio: Ken lives in Pennsylvania and hunts with an Equinox 900, Deus II, and Nokta Legend. His finds have been featured in numerous books, newspapers, and magazines in the United States, England, and Germany. He feels honored to have donated recovered coins and relics to museums in both the United States and England. Ken is the owner of the popular site Detectorist.com/Detectorists.com and is also the author of this book.

Find Info: Recovered in March 2018 in Shropshire, England, this coin, along with two others I found, is part of the "Shropshire Short Cross Hoard," which now totals 46 coins. All the coins were donated to a museum in England.

"Shropshire Short Cross Hoard" Silver Penny (1189–1216)

LISA STANCO

Bio: Lisa is from Schenectady, New York. She started metal detecting in 2010, and relics are her favorite items to find. She feels there is something really special about pulling an item from the dirt and being the first person to look at it in centuries. Lisa currently uses an XP Deus II and an Equinox 800.

Find Info: USA buttons were the most universally used military-marked buttons worn by the Continental Army during the Revolutionary War. It is a piece of history from the War of American Independence and was once worn by one of America's first heroes. Unearthing it was the thrill of a lifetime.

USA Continental Army
General Service, Pewter Button

MARC HOOVER

Bio: Marc is from Altamonte Springs, Florida, and uses a Garrett AT Pro and Minelab Equinox 800. Marc is the creator and founder of the Adventures In History Facebook group. His article on the recovery of Spanish treasure on a Florida beach, titled "Tragedy, Triumph, and Treasure," won the Freelance Writer's Freedom Award for 2021 in American Digger Magazine (Vol. 17, Issue 2). For Marc's full bio, visit adventuresinhistory.com.

Find Info: "Ed Pinaud Paris" ornate bottle with a silver thimble-like screw-on top. It was recovered at an old gold mining ghost town, Quartzburg, Idaho, in the summer of 2017. This town was destroyed by a catastrophic fire in 1938, and almost all the glass in town was either shattered or melted due to the intense heat. This fully intact bottle from the early 1900s is a hair tonic bottle, probably from the town's barbershop.

Ed Pinaud Paris
Ornate Bottle With Silver Top

MATTHEW HARDING

Bio: Matthew Harding is from Mountville, Pennsylvania, and he hunts with the Minelab Equinox 800. He is the secretary for the Lancaster Research and Recovery Club and a member of The Ring Finders. Matthew shares his adventures and finds on his YouTube channel, "The Lanco History Saver." Having a direct connection to history has always intrigued him.

Find Info: My favorite find is a 14k gold men's wedding band. Estimated age from late 1700's to early 1800's based on location found and structure of the ring.

Men's Wedding Ring 14K Gold
1700s–1800s

PAM POPP

Bio: Pam Popp lives in St. Charles, Missouri, and hunts with a Minelab Equinox 800. She often travels to Colchester, England, to metal detect with her husband, Tim. Pam belongs to the Midwest Coinshooters and Historical Club and Gateway Metal Detecting.

Find Info: My favorite find is a silver buckle I found in Poughkeepsie, New York, in 1989 with my first metal detector, a Minelab Sovereign. I have been hooked ever since, and I always wonder who last held something I have found.

Silver Shoe Buckle

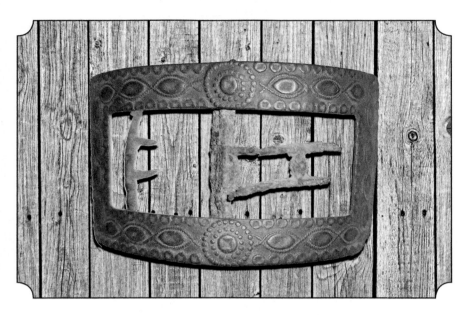

RICH SWOGER

Bio: Rich Swoger, from Aliquippa, Pennsylvania, hunts with an XP Deus detector. Rich took part in "Dig it with KG and Ringy" at Metal Detecting Holidays in the UK in 2018 and 2019. He enjoys bottle digging and organized hunts such as D.I.V. and the Charles Garrett Memorial Hunt.

Find Info: This powder flask is my favorite find so far because it is so unique. They are not found very often and are just a cool piece of history. It was found near an old cellar hole in the woods of Western Pennsylvania. These flasks were used from about 1800 until metallic cartridges became popular in the 1870s.

Copper Black Powder Flask
With Hunting Scene

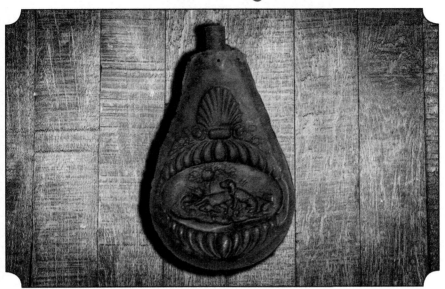

RICK LESQUIER

Bio: Rick is 68 years old and from Somerset, Kentucky. He has been detecting since he was 14 and uses a Minelab CTX 3030. Rick enjoys hunting beaches, parks, farms, woods, and old home sites.

Find Info: Roman Fibula Brooch from 100–200 AD, Ponden Hill type. Recovered in Shropshire, England, in March 2018, more than 18" deep on a very cold and snowy day! Considering this brooch was in the ground for almost 1800 years, it's in wonderful condition! Beautiful decoration on the neck, and amazingly, the spring and pin (unbroken) are still in place too!

Roman Fibula Brooch
100- 200AD

ROBIN KYNASTON

Bio: Having lived his whole life in Shropshire, a region nestled on the border of England and Wales, Rob has been surrounded by an abundant historical legacy that stretches back thousands of years. With such a captivating backdrop on his doorstep, it is only natural that his venture into metal detecting has led to a series of awe-inspiring finds right from the very beginning.

Find Info: My favorite find is my Henry VI silver Half Groat from 1422–1461, with a London mint. It was found in Shropshire, England, with the Garrett AT Pro.

1422-1461 Henry VI
Silver Half Groat

SHAWN SHERRILL

Bio: Shawn "SGT Whitey" Sherrill is from Mansfield, Arkansas and currently resides in Raleigh, North Carolina. Shawn has used Whites, Garrett, and XP metal detectors. He is currently the President of Wake County Metal Detecting club (WCMDclub.com) and can be found on Facebook at @Wake County Metal Detecting (PUBLIC).

Find Info: Super rare Civil War Ohio Breast Plate that was dug in Harpers Ferry, West Virginia, at an Ohio Union Camp site. We have found almost 1,000 bullets, several buttons, and many other Civil War relics. It's the rarest of all Union breastplates.

Civil War
Ohio Breast Plate

SIAN HARRISON

Bio: Born and raised in Wrexham, North Wales, Sian has been metal detecting since 2022. She uses the Garrett Euroace and has already found some amazing things. As a primary school teacher, Sian often brings her finds to share with her students, who are amazed to hold such pieces of history.

Find Info: Silver Trajan Denarius. Arabia and Camel. Obverse: IMP TRAIANO AVG GER DAC P M TR P. Laureate bust right, with slight drapery. Reverse: COS V P P S P Q R OPTIMO PRINC. Arabia standing left, holding branch and bundle of cinnamon sticks, behind to left, camel advancing left. RIC 142. Rome mint, ca. AD 110.

Silver Trajan Denarius
110AD

TERRY SHANNON

Bio: Winter resident of Melbourne Beach, Florida, Terry prefers using the XP Deus II and Nokta Legend detectors. He has written and published five books on metal detecting, all of which are available on Amazon and his website, terryshannon.com. Terry has also been a guest speaker at various Metal Detecting clubs, featured on several podcasts, and interviewed for numerous Facebook metal detecting channels.

Find Info: My favorite find is one of the oldest coins found on the Treasure Coast: a 1544 Carlos & Joanna four reale Spanish coin. The coin was identified to be from the assayer Juan Gutierrez, who worked from 1544-1548.

Carlos & Joanna Four Reale
1544–1548

TIM BLANK

Bio: Tim lives in Northern Illinois and goes by "Ill Digger" on his YouTube channel and Instagram page. He has been metal detecting since 2009 and has detected in 16 states and 4 countries. Tim uses a Minelab Equinox 800 and XP Deus II.

Find Info: My favorite find is the ancient gold ingot I found while I was detecting near Colchester, England, in October of 2018. The ingot weighs just under 3 ounces and is currently in the possession of the British Museum. It dates between the late Roman and early Medieval time periods and is the second largest gold ingot found in isolation in Britain!

Ancient Gold Ingot
81.54 Grams

TIM POPP

Bio: Tim Popp is from St. Charles, Missouri. He hunts with a Minelab Equinox 800 or CTX3030. He is the Treasurer of Midwest Coinshooters and Historical Club in St. Louis, Missouri. Tim enjoys meeting and hunting with other detectorists and the anticipation of the next piece of history to come out of the ground. Tim and his wife have traveled to England three times to metal detect.

Find Info: 1560-1561 Queen Elizabeth 1st hammered silver shilling (12 pence) with a Martlet mint mark. Recovered in September 2022 in Colchester, England.

1560-1 Queen Elizabeth 1st Hammered Silver Shilling

TIM SAYLOR

Bio: Tim Saylor (aka Ringmaster Tim), of National Geographic's "DIGGERS" and the Pursuit channel's "DIGGIN with KG & RINGY," has been a treasure hunter for over 30 years. As part of Team Garrett, he and his TV co-star King George continue to search for treasures worldwide, with multiple museum contributions in England, Europe, and the USA. Their exploits, documented in over 85 television shows, countless YouTube videos, touring events, and a live podcast series, can all be referenced at DIGGINTV.com.

Find Info: 1744 gold mourning ring with an amethyst stone, found with a Garrett AT MAX using a large MGC coil. An incredible piece of history, logged and loaned to the renowned Hill family museum in England, and featured in the "Golden Ring" episode of TV's DIGGIN with KG & RINGY.

Gold Mourning Ring
1744

TODD YERKS

Bio: Todd Yerks, aka CT Todd, is an avid detectorist with over 25 years of experience in the fields and woods of the northeastern United States. He is also a Barn Leader for the Colchester Group in England and leads yearly trips. He maintains a personal website featuring his finds, machine settings, permission tips, and cleaning tips to assist other detectorists. Visit CTTODD.com.

Find Info: I found this Claddagh-style gold ring in a cornfield outside of a small cemetery. It has both a 1700s hallmark and the owner's initials, "ED". The ring was made by Cornelius Wynkoop, a silversmith from NYC between 1724 and 1741, making it a true treasure, a Colonial Gold Ring!

Colonial Gold Ring
1724-1741

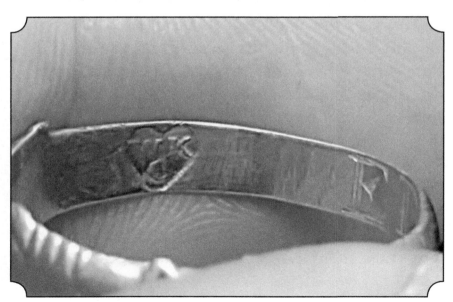

WENDY HETHERINGTON

Bio: Wendy lives in Welland, Ontario, Canada, and began metal detecting in 2007 with her husband, Jeff. She prefers to use an XP Deus Lite when detecting. As a Scout leader, she has introduced numerous young people to this hobby.

Find Info: The first really old coin I recovered was found in an old pub field in England. This hammered silver penny features the famous Virgin Queen, Queen Elizabeth I, and was minted in London between 1573 and 1577.

Queen Elizabeth I
1573-1577

WILLIAM BARKER

Bio: William Barker is based on the Isle of Skye on the west coast of Scotland, UK. He has been detecting for 7 years and uses a Garrett Euro ACE. William is proud to have a treasure case with a beautiful medieval gold and amethyst stirrup ring! Will goes nowhere without his trusty sidekick and lucky charm, Sonic the terrier!

Find Info: 1683 Charles II Silver Maundy 3 Pence is a fine example of one of the first milled coins to be regularly minted in the United Kingdom and marked the end of Britain's silver hammered coinage. It's quite an elusive coin to find for most detectorists in the UK!

1683 Charles II
Silver Maundy 3 Pence

Printed in Great Britain
by Amazon

34041351R00069